MW01480002

THE **HIGHLY EFFECTIVE DRIVING INSTRUCTOR**

SECRET KEYS TO A SUCCESSFUL DRIVER TRAINING

BY **VOLNY DORCÉUS** B.Ed

Tellwell Talent
www.tellwell.ca

ISBN
978-1-77370-643-6 (Hardcover)
978-1-77370-642-9 (Paperback)
978-1-77370-644-3 (eBook)

This book is dedicated to my lovely wife, Jessy:
the best friend, wife, mother and partner,
and to the colleagues, students and parents
who allowed me to drive with their children. You are
the lifeblood of the driver-training industry.

TABLE OF CONTENTS

ACKNOWLEDGEMENTS

Thank you to:

Ken Pike, who evaluated me as a driver and started training me so that I could become a driving instructor.

Barry Fizer, who helped me finish the instructor training modules.

Cliff Skidmore, who was the first to tell me I would become an excellent instructor.

Jessy Joseph, my wife and office assistant, who helps support my dream of operating a driver training school.

INTRODUCTION

At the time of this writing, I have been teaching Driver Education in the province of Alberta, Canada for ten years. During that journey I have learned a whole lot. I only started this career to get some extra money to help my wife pay a few bills while I was working toward a bachelor's degree in education.

At that time, I discovered my passion for helping others get to a point they needed to be in their lives. When they obtained their driver's license, their whole life changed. They could accept an offer for a job they really needed in order to feed their families, or pay their apartment's rent or their mortgages.

Briefly stated, they got another lease on life. And, so did I. They say that you can never help others without helping yourself, in one way or another.

During those ten years, I have encountered many teachers:

- The two instructors who trained me to become a driving instructor.

- The Alberta Transportation examiner who tested me and gave me the opportunity to serve Alberta in a different capacity than before.

- The parents who gave me the privilege of working with their children.

- The many men and women who allowed me to work with their spouses.

- My fellow driving instructors with whom I worked—the ones I personally trained and those who had already acquired their instructor's licenses before we worked together.

- Last, but not least: life in general, which threw at me whatever lessons I needed to acquire in order to become the driving instructor I am today.

I strongly believe that this book will provide many insights on the world of driver training to the public in general, but most importantly to:

- The parents, so they have a better understanding of Driver Education when they enroll their child.

- The students, so they know what to expect when dealing with a driving instructor.

- My fellow driving instructors, who work in the field of driver training and who do not earn a good living at it yet.

In conclusion, I want this book to become part of my legacy in the world of driver training. I have been given so much. I learned, I earned and now I want to return some of what I have been given. That's my way of adding value to you, the reader.

Enjoy it!
Volny

CHAPTER 1

How to become a driving instructor in Alberta

If you had asked me this question ten years ago, I would have answered you this way: you have your driver's license, you have been driving for some time and you have a car. Well, place an ad in the paper and wait for your phone to ring. Let your friends know that you are in the business of teaching people how to drive, and you are set.

Well, I would have been wrong. If it was done this way, it would be easy to be in the Driver Education business. Actually, in the province of Alberta, we do have many people who operate like that in the cities and towns where I have been. According to Alberta Transportation, it is illegal to provide driver training for a fee without having a proper instructor's license from the government.

Driver Education is regulated in the province of Alberta and I am glad it is that way. Anyone desiring to become a professional driving instructor must possess a driving instructor's license and, at the same time, that instructor must be attached to a driving school licensed by Alberta Transportation.

These are the requirements, as outlined by the government of Alberta. If you want to become a driving instructor:

- You must hold an operator's license not cancelled or suspended under the criminal code of Canada during the 5 years preceding your application.

- Your driving record must be satisfactory to the registrar for the 2 years preceding the date of your application.

- You must provide proof of a criminal record check acceptable to the registrar, obtained from a municipal service or RCMP (Royal Canadian Mounted Police) detachment and dated to within 90 days of the application.

- You must have no outstanding fines.

- You must pass a required training by Alberta Transportation. Alberta-licensed driver training schools are the only ones approved to provide such training.

- When all training is complete and you have passed your instructor tests, you must pay your instructor license fee, service charges and any other applicable fees at a registry agent's office, and submit proof of payment to Alberta Transportation.

◆ In our case, the candidate for a class 5 instructor's license must be a holder of a class 1, 2 or 4 driver's license for at least 3 years before the application is made.

If you require up-to-date information, please contact a Driver Programs Administrator at:

Alberta Transportation
Driver Programs and Licensing Standards
Room 109, 4999 – 98 Ave, NW
Edmonton, AB, T6B 2X3
Telephone: 780-427-8901
Fax: 780-427-0833

Or,

Alberta Transportation
Driver Programs and Licensing Standards
1st floor, 803 Manning Road NE
Calgary, AB, T2E 7M8
Telephone: 403-297-6679

Also, driving instructors must renew their instructor's license every two years and they have to satisfy the same requirements that they did before they received their initial license. In other words, the government is keeping a close eye on all licensed driving instructors.

In Alberta, we do have a good number of licensed driving instructors. They are mostly concentrated in two major cities: Calgary and Edmonton. More than half of the existing schools are located in those two cities as well, according to data provided by the government in 2014.

If you live in a state or territory, or a province other than Alberta, please contact the department of motor vehicles of your area for information on how you can become a licensed driving instructor.

CHAPTER 2

Why become a licensed driving instructor?

Upsides of becoming a driving instructor (the answers will vary for different people):

THE DESIRE TO HELP OTHERS ACQUIRE THEIR DRIVER'S LICENSE

When you provide driver training, you are in the business of caring, of helping other people. You must not only have a passion for it, but also the desire to help others more than you want to help yourself.

Yes, you want to provide driving instruction, but your real pay is the smile you see on their face, and the confidence they exhibit in themselves when they pass the driver's road test. You can witness that in the way they walk and in the way they talk.

Nothing brings more joy than when you see a student of yours—say, a welfare recipient—pass their road test on Thursday, go for a job interview on Friday, then get the job and drive to work on Monday. There are times some ladies look so beautiful on their way to work that you don't even recognize them. If you pay attention, when they thank you for helping them to get a better shot at life you will witness one of its most beautiful moments.

If you were born to teach, if you were born to do Driver's Education, you will be well-rewarded for it.

It is a fact that some people are more naturally suited to being in a helping profession than others. If you do not know your personality style, it is well worth the effort to attend some training so you can learn more about yourself. The training will help you decide whether or not you are a good candidate for a driver training career (or *calling*, if you prefer).

Later on, I will give you a brief overview of a personality training that I have attended in Atlanta, Georgia, USA. Dr. Robert Rohm from Personality Insights trained us in the DISC model of human behavior.

In brief,

- The "D" stands for "Dominant"—someone who likes to be in charge.
- The "I" stands for "Inspiring"—someone who likes to have fun.

- The "S" stands for "Supportive"—someone who likes to support, to help.

- The "C" stands for "Cautious"—someone who likes to follow methods and procedures.

In the teaching profession, I have met many people with high "C" and high "S" personality traits, and some with high "D" or high "I" personality traits. I will talk more about the DISC model of human behavior later in this book. If you want to know more about DISC, please consider attending a training offered by one of the DISC consultants in your country, or, if you live in the province of Alberta, I would be happy to have you in one of my DISC trainings.

THE POSSIBILITY OF EARNING EXTRA INCOME

You will certainly encounter instructors from varied walks of life who provide driver education so they can earn an extra income.

Many are retirees. Driver training schools love them, since work is mostly after school and on weekends, and retirees don't mind that. It is another way for them to serve their communities and to get out of their houses to earn some cash.

Adult students provide driver education as well, once they are done taking university classes for the day or when they have no classes at all, or on weekends and during summer vacations. They do their best to balance their work life and their university life.

There are also people who work at other professions who work part time in the driver training business as well.

IT IS A WAY OF LIFE, AND THE ONLY SOURCE OF INCOME

When it is your only source of income, chances are you will be more committed to driver education. As the saying goes: "A lot of things will come your way, the moment you make a commitment."

Lots of driving schools prefer workers who are available all day but it does not mean they have work for you all the time, yet you are left on stand-by.

Once you are available, you can travel more, from one town to the next, in order to serve your customers, which means less downtime. But for that to happen, you must be 100% committed.

THE DESIRE TO BECOME ONE'S OWN BOSS

It is an excellent way to create your own job or to overcome a recent layoff or firing. Some of us are more inclined to that desire (or are forced to), but most of us are not. We just need a job that pays us well.

Before you can be your own boss in Alberta, you must first have your driving school license. And before you can even apply for that license you must work for a driver training school in Alberta for at least two years, and then satisfy all the requirements of the registrar at Alberta Transportation.

You may have the desire to become your own boss because you were either fired or laid off, and lost your main source of income. Bear in mind that opening your own driving school means you will have to deal with people, get your own customers, do your own advertising and scheduling, and so on. It is not as easy as many people think. But you can do it, and you must be a lifelong learner.

THE OPPORTUNITY TO MEET NEW PEOPLE, EXPERIENCE NEW CULTURES AND VISIT NEW PLACES IN ALBERTA

Dr. John C. Maxwell wrote: "Working with people means there is no guarantee of smooth sailing." Many world cultures live and work in Alberta. To become a highly effective driving instructor, you will need to be savvy about the different personality styles present in different people, and also be aware of your own per-sonality style and know how to interact with others.

It would be nice to know more languages than English. If you don't, you could be at a disadvantage.

Knowing more than one language could help increase business for you. If you don't think so, ask your fellow driving instructors who speak two, three, four or more different languages (in addition to French and English) and hear what they will tell you, and then you will know for yourself.

You may also have to become more culturally sensitive. Certain cultures do certain things in certain ways. They want your instruction and you want their money.

As the late Zig Ziglar used to say: "If you help enough people get what they want, they can help you get almost anything you want." Mistakes or weaknesses in your relationships with others can cost you thousands of dollars, or your career.

I have met many individuals who lack people skills and who transferred jobs to become driving examiners, or moved on to other fields. In summary, leave nothing to chance. As Brian Tracy said: "

Everything counts. It can either help or hurt you. Nothing is neutral."

You will have the offer to travel to new places around Alberta. You should welcome those opportunities, they are great. When I have eight to ten people to train in a two- to three-week period, I just stay at a hotel, do the work and come back home with lots of money in my bank account.

DOWNSIDES OF BECOMING A DRIVING INSTRUCTOR:

THE PAY CAN BE LOW WHEN HOURS OF INSTRUCTION ARE FEW

Certain driving schools, especially those that have been in business for a while, do not pay as well as they claim to. Remember, you provide the car and you are responsible for all costs associated with insurance and the operation of that motor vehicle in the province or state that you are working. That is why they call you a contractor. You are also responsible to pay for your own taxes and contribute to your own retirement plan.

If you are an employee, your pay will be extremely low. By the way, driver training schools hire very few of them, if any at all. It is not cost-effective to hire employees.

YOU PROVIDE INSTRUCTION ONLY WHEN STUDENTS ARE AVAILABLE

It is not a 9 to 5 job. Therefore, you are expected to work whenever customers are available, so you are always on call. At Saint Paul Driving School we hire driving contractors. The towns in which we operate are far apart from each other. Consequently, we offer our contractors 75% of the fees we charge. As an example, our customers pay us $60 per hour and we pay $45 per hour to our contractors. When customers pay more, we pay more to our contractors as well. So it is a win-win for all of us.

We do not pay for travel time. And if students cancel on you, it will be an issue. Most parents don't want to pay extra fees and we cannot afford to compensate for that. Once in a while we will help, but we do not have unlimited funds.

Since we have the hours, the fees we pay to our contractors allow them to cover their expenses with plenty left over to take care of themselves and their families.

There are times we travel onto reserves in Alberta. Any contractor who is willing to travel with us gets a better piece of the action. Our clients pay us more so we can afford to pay more. And we have yet to see another driving school that can match or surpass what we provide in terms of compensation to our contractors. Again, we operate Saint Paul Driving School.

WEEKEND WORK OR HOLIDAY WORK MAY BE REQUIRED BY A DRIVING SCHOOL

At our school, we do not operate on Saturdays for both religious and personal reasons.

For other driving schools, you may be required to work on weekends and holidays as well. Students are not in school on Saturdays and Sundays, during holidays or on professional development days for teachers.

I have noticed more driving school cars on the road on Saturdays but a very few on Sundays.

If you cannot work on Saturdays for personal or religious reasons, please let your company know. Hopefully, they can accommodate you. After all, you only get paid when you work.

NO BENEFITS, SICK LEAVE, FAMILY LEAVE OR PAID VACATIONS

There are absolutely no benefits offered when you are a contractor—no sick leave, family leave or paid vacations at all. You don't get paid for holidays, either. And if you provide driving instruction during holidays, you get the same hourly pay for your services as non-holiday days.

If you take time off during the Christmas season, Easter or summer, remember that you will receive no payment for those occasions. I suggest that you work more hours when you can and budget your money.

OWNING YOUR OWN VEHICLE IS REQUIRED TO PROVIDE INSTRUCTION

You must have your own vehicle. Dealerships will not lease you a vehicle if they know you are going to provide driving instruction. When you purchase a vehicle, you must have driver training endorsement with your insurance company. Which means you will pay more for your insurance. For example, I pay three times as much for my driver training car than I do for my personal vehicle.

(Disclaimer: this job is only for those with a passion for helping others.)

NO PAID MILEAGE

There is absolutely no payment for picking up and dropping off students. You only get paid for face-time with your customers. If you want to get paid more money, then increase your face-time with your customers and rent your car to the students when they are ready to go for their road tests.

NO PAYMENT WHEN YOUR CAR IS IN THE SHOP

You are not working when your car is in the shop for service. Make sure you have the money to pay the bill, too, so you can get your car out of the shop. The driving school that you provide your services to is not generous enough to help you pay for maintenance.

THERE'S LOTS OF DOWNTIME

During your reading, I will explain to you how to make sure you only have minimal downtime and what you can do in order to earn decent money all year round. I have gained annual results in sales of well over one hundred thousand dollars, year after year. In order to do that, you will have to travel around and do what I did (or do better than I did) to experience those results. I will share my successes with you so you can duplicate them. I will also share my failures with you so you can do your best to avoid them.

I have lost thousands of dollars because some customers did not pay me, and also because some fellow instructors dropped the ball on countless occasions.

THERE IS LESS WORK IN THE WINTER

Winter is a wonderful and interesting season. It gets dark early. In general, you will drive with one student after school each work day. If you travel to more than one town, you have a chance of teaching adults during the day as well. And if you get a good hourly rate, six hours per day (or a minimum of 30 hours per week) will be helpful to you.

If you work in a big city and the driving school you work for is already successful, chances are you will get decent hours of work. It is difficult to estimate the income you can expect, since reliable data is not readily available in this industry. Reminder, you have to be committed and available full-time to earn some money.

You've got to provide superior driving instruction. Your service should be second-to-none, and the public will reward you handsomely. This is the hallmark of a highly effective driving instructor.

CHAPTER 3

The job of a driving instructor

In the province of Alberta; Canada, under its occupational profile, "driving instructor" is also known as "auto driving instructor," "educator," "instructor" or "teacher."

The driving instructor teaches the "knowledge and skills required to safely operate vehicles such as cars, motorcycles, transport trucks and buses." Some instructors work both in-classroom and in-car. Others work in the classroom only, but most instructors prefer to teach in-car lessons.

PERSONAL QUALITIES
REQUIRED FOR THE JOB:

- ◆ Patience and calmness.

- ◆ The ability to get along with all kinds of people.

- ◆ Good communication and teaching skills.

- ◆ The ability to instill confidence in others.

REQUIRED EDUCATION:

In Alberta, I have met driving instructors with different levels of education: non-high school graduates as well as high school graduates. Some have bachelor's and master's degrees. To my great surprise, I met one instructor who holds a doctorate degree. He has other people working for him at his school. He oversees the operations and still continues to meet the requirements so that he can renew his instructor's license. He also earns extra income doing consulting work via his doctorate training.

In order to provide driver training in Alberta for pay, you must be licensed by Alberta Transportation. If you live in a province other than Alberta, or if you live in the United States, you must contact your local Department of Motor Vehicles to find out what is required to become a driving instructor.

One thing is guaranteed: the more you are trained on how to train others and the more knowledge you have in the field of human behavior, the better your job will be as a driving instructor.

Simply put, the highly effective driving instructor learns more to earn more.

Dr. Robert A. Rohm wrote a great blog post on personality-insights.com: "To earn more, you must learn more." I have taken a few excerpts from it for your consideration.

TIP: TO EARN MORE, YOU MUST LEARN MORE!

"Whether you realize it or not, you are in a position to earn more income than you are presently receiving. It will require a little thought and energy on your part but it will be well worth the effort."

"In order to earn more than you presently make, you must learn some things that you do not currently know. People who are making huge sums of money are not better than you. They are not smarter than you, nor are they more special than you. However, they do know a few things that you do not know. That is why they earn the money they do. You see, they have become an expert in a specific area of life so they are being rewarded for learning the information they have received. You see, they are getting paid more because they learned to think more."

"Additional knowledge greatly increases your earning power because you begin to see that the issue is not how smart you are but rather how committed you are to learning new information."

"I do not believe that it is necessary for you to become a world renowned [sic] scholar in a particular area to be successful, but if you do learn a great deal about a specific topic, it will not be long before people will be coming to you for advice and counsel. Then you will be in a position to increase your financial picture."

"When you stay focused and grow in a particular area, it will not be long before you become one of the leaders in that field".

CHAPTER 4

Working for a driving school

Your career as a driving instructor starts as soon as you pass your driving instructor's test and receive your driving instructor's license from the government.

When I started this career, I was the fifteenth instructor hired at the school. This means that, as an instructor, I got work after my fourteen colleagues got work, or I was handed the difficult students that no one wanted to work with. Needless to say, there was very little work available to me so it was financially difficult at first.

I had bought a brand-new car in order to provide driving instruction to my students. The car payment was three hundred and ninety-five dollars per month. The insurance payment on my driver training car was one hundred and ninety-five dollars per month. I lived eighty kilometers away from the city I was assigned to. Therefore, the round trip was one hundred and sixty kilometers.

My first pay was eight hundred and forty dollars for the first month, five hundred for the second month. And I had no students booked on my schedule for the following month. The inevitable happened. I stopped offering my services to the school.

Now that I had an extra car and extra insurance to pay, I ended up working for a fast-food restaurant on my free time and I also delivered flyers and newspapers for a local newspaper company. The following summer I called another driving school. They could not believe I was ready to go and had no one to provide instruction to. I was hired as a contractor on the same day and I started to provide instruction the day after that.

It was the month of July when I joined the second driving school. I earned five times more than I did contracting for the first school. Therefore, I had plenty of money to pay the bills with some to spare. When September came I went back to university to complete the third year of my Bachelor of Education degree, with a specialization in business and French. I taught driver's education in the afternoon and on Sundays. Sometimes, when I had no class in the morning, I helped students as needed.

When I was awarded my education degree I was hired as a French teacher. In total, I was with the second driving school for about a year and a half. The school owner gave me all the information I needed to apply for a driving school license. Six months later, the school license came through the mail.

At the beginning, you will be excited. You'll get to train all kinds of students:

STUDENTS WITH LESSER AMOUNT OF EDUCATION

You need to be patient with them. They will need more practice. Make sure you let their parents or guardians know so they can budget enough money for you to get the job done so the students can obtain their driver's license.

STUDENTS WITH GREATER AMOUNT OF EDUCATION

These people have already done so much learning in their lives. Learning to drive will be just another easy task for them. They are ready for it. You should have a wonderful time teaching them.

STUDENTS WITH LIMITED OR NO ENGLISH KNOWLEDGE AT ALL

During my career, I have worked with students who spoke my native language. It was easy to work with them.

Other students had limited knowledge of English and spoke only French, so I spoke French while working with them, but they had to memorize the driving maneuvers in English because that was the only language the examiners spoke.

I had three students once who only spoke Spanish. As I was the only one on staff who spoke their language, I worked with them. Again, those Spanish speakers had to memorize the driving maneuvers in English. They still passed their driving road test.

If you only speak English as an instructor, it does not mean you can't teach students who speak another language, but I personally think that the language barrier will be an issue. The stress level of those students will be at an all-time high.

I once had a Chinese student. She spoke no English at all, and I don't speak Chinese. Luckily for me, her husband had driven with her many times before and I only had to do four hours of driving lessons with her. I used gestures for left turns and right turns, and for going straight. The parking maneuvers were all numbered and I had her husband explain them to her before we got into the car. Then we were good to go. She did well, and later obtained her driver's license. I would not mind repeating the experience, but I would prefer that the student speaks English.

I had another experience with a student from a different country. He barely knew English, and we had a very close call while driving. Another driver almost hit us on the driver's side (the student's side of my vehicle), which would not have been good for my record as a driving instructor.

We agreed on a speed of 10 km/hour when going through a yield sign, and my student also needed to check left and right and left again before crossing the intersection. He was travelling at 36 km/

hour, and did not slow down and did not check the intersection. I pointed at the speedometer and told we need "10," and I showed him my ten fingers. He thought that I said "turn," so he decided to turn right. In the meantime, a driver was coming from our left side and spotted my student making a right turn from the center of the road. I grabbed the wheel with my left hand, braked slowly and brought the car to the right side of the road.

The left-side driver saw what was happening. She must have slowed down quickly, since she did not hit us. While we stayed by the curbside, she went on her way. We would have been in the wrong if we had got hit. I asked my student to tell me what happened, and how we could avoid being in a situation like that the next time. He was calm, gave a good explanation and off we went with our driving lesson.

You've got to be extra cautious when you work with someone with a limited knowledge of English, as the potential for misunderstanding is extremely high. As a highly effective driving instructor you have to know how to work with everyone, and it will expand your experience. I am so privileged that driver training provides me with an opportunity to work with students from different nations around the world. I can make a global impact right where I live.

STUDENTS WHO ARE
NATIVE ENGLISH SPEAKERS

They have been speaking English all their life, so you should not have any problems understanding them. If you are their instructor and they have difficulty understanding you, I hope they have mercy on you. Treat your students well, and with the utmost respect and they will give you a chance. Demonstrate to them what to do and they will do it. Speak less and let them practice the driving maneuvers over and over again. They will learn fast and they will thank you for it.

A lot of us driving instructors had to learn English as a second language. I started learning English when I was thirteen years old and in junior high school, two to three hours per week. That training continued until I graduated from high school, and then I went to the United States for university training and enrolled at the Intensive English Institute located on the campus of the University of Maine in Orono, Maine. One semester later I was immersed in full classes, and then graduated with a degree in business.

A few years later, I enrolled at Husson University in Bangor, Maine, USA, and attended classes in computer information systems for the three years prior to moving to Canada with my wife and two children. After living in Quebec for four years we moved to Alberta and I enrolled in an education degree program, which I mentioned earlier. At the time that I am writing this book, I have been a class 5 driving instructor for at least ten years. Once in a while, one of my students will say to me: "Some people said you have an accent, but I understand you perfectly," to which I reply, "Thank you. All of us have an accent. Mine is different than yours and I am glad it is that way. Let's continue with driving."

Remember, your goal is to be a highly effective driving instructor. As such, you must do your best to please your customers. No matter what you do, you will not be able to please them all. As the saying goes: "You can please some of the people some of the time, but you cannot please all of the people all of the time."

Be the highly effective driving instructor you were meant to be!

STUDENTS WITH LEARNING DISABILITIES

As long as a student obtains his or her learner's license, I strongly believe they can learn how to drive. Some students may have difficulty reading, but learn better hands-on. If this is the case, they will have no problems in learning how to drive.

Alberta Transportation recommends at least 60 hours of practice before a student attempts to take the road test. In other words, students need to practice a lot. If they have learning disabilities they will require extra driving practice. They can do so with members of their families.

Your responsibility as a driving instructor is to inform the parents or guardians in advance that a student with a learning disability will need enormous hours of driving practice. They may not want to pay extra, which is fine.

I remember two cases I had recently...

The first case had to do with a young woman who inherited a four hundred thousand dollar house and three hundred thousand dollars in cash from her mother. This lady decided to change her life by learning how to drive. She told me she had learning disabilities and already had her learner's license. I drove the first hour with her and decided that we would drive together one hour at a time. In total, we drove ten hours.

She had practiced a bit with her mother before she passed away, but she said her mother was not the greatest teacher. After her driving sessions with me, she took the road test and failed. The following week she went to take the test again.

Then, one day, I saw someone driving a nice vehicle beside me. The driver waved at me, and I saw that it was the young woman! I concluded that if she was driving by herself, chances are she had passed the road test. A few minutes later I sent her a text message, and she replied to inform me of her success, and that she was legally able to drive by herself. I congratulated her and asked her to keep on driving safely.

The second case was also another woman, I will keep her name private as well. Her case worker warned us of a learning disability and could not disclose more information. The first time we drove for two hours and she was very afraid. We had to pull over several times to let other drivers pass. One time, I remember telling her: "Just imagine you have a date with your boyfriend and you would not want to keep him waiting. How often would you pull over and let other vehicles pass?" She said that she would not pull over at all. So, I said: "Let's pretend that today is the day you have the date with your boyfriend and let us not stop for any oncoming traffic." She never stopped again until we had finished the lesson, and never stopped during subsequent lessons, either.

To help her keep her calm when we drove, we only did one-hour sessions thereafter. We drove fourteen hours altogether. Then her case worker booked her road test for 12:45 p.m. It was lunch time, which meant it could be quite busy. We reviewed our driving procedures that day, and before she left I mentioned to her: "Today is the day. You can do it. Today is the day to get your driver's license so you can go pick up your boyfriend for that date we were talking about when you started. Remember, you can do this."

She drove away in the driver training car, with the examiner in the passenger seat. When they returned she exited the car, and you could see her self-confidence in the way she was walking and smiling. It was merely a formality when she told me that she had passed. Her body language had already leaked out the entire message.

I do not need to be warned about a student's learning disability. My personal philosophy is that if they can confidently pass their learner's test, I can confidently help them learn how to drive.

In the driver training business, remember that the more difficult the students are, and the more you learn about your own personal growth, the closer you are to becoming a highly effective driving instructor.

DEALING WITH GIFTED STUDENTS

Some of us may think that a gifted student is one who has a high intelligence quotient (IQ), someone who is gifted academically. Yes, I am privileged to work with students who are gifted this way, but for some reason, they are usually just OK drivers. But they have their life already set out for them in the academic world and we should be fine with that. We need them to serve humanity in their chosen profession.

During my driver training career, I have encountered those who are naturally gifted drivers. The general public may not consider this, but I noticed it. These drivers may not do well in school, but when you place them behind the wheel they are right at home. They are very comfortable, and quickly learn how to drive with very little instruction. When you ask them if they have ever driven before, they will usually say: "No, I watched what you did and I just followed what you told me to do." Pay attention to those drivers when they arrive, you are in the presence of greatness. Those individuals will have a profound impact on you. They are the best drivers you will ever work with.

We have also had students who live on farms. They are not all great drivers, be watchful of them as well. Those who have already been on a tractor or an air seeder already know how to drive. There will not be much to teach them except safety issues; uphill, downhill and parallel parking and safe highway driving.

Again, be extra cautious because some of them would definitely qualify to become a Formula One or NASCAR driver. These boys and girls really love to drive fast. Sometimes—after repeated requests to slow down after they reached 130 km/hour on the highway—I sincerely wished I had an eject button that I could push to get them out of my car before they killed me.

When I started teaching, I had limited life insurance. When these student behaviors continued to occur, I went to my insurance agent and increased my life insurance so that I could continue to provide for my underage children if something disastrous happened. If you have people who depend on you and whose life will be affected if you are not there, you should consider buying insurance, or increasing your life insurance if you already have some. This is only my opinion, of course.

When you encounter those super-fast drivers, be ready to put lots of mileage on your car. The only way you can keep them engaged is by keeping them driving. If I have to do ten hours with them for the insurance discount: 10 hours of driving plus classroom instruction so the students can pay a lower insurance premium in Alberta; I only drive three times with them. If their parents want me to verify that they are ready for their road test, I will teach them what they need to know in a two-hour session, and then I send them away with love. That's my way of getting rid of them fast before they kill me.

STUDENTS WITH DIFFERENT PERSONALITY STYLES

I was privileged to attend a leadership conference organized by the John Maxwell Team in Orlando, Florida. At that conference, we met Dr. Robert A. Rohm, a guest speaker, and he talked to us about the DISC Model of Human Behavior. We had quite an interesting time with him. Then he gave us the opportunity to register for more training so we could become DISC trainers or consultants.

A few months later, I joined Dr. Rohm in Atlanta, Georgia where he trained us so that we can train others to learn about their personality style, and how their style interacts with others. From that time on, I never saw myself or others in the same way again. That training revolutionized my personal life, and I began to approach my work life in a whole new way. What a discovery that was! I saw the world around me through a new set of lenses.

I am going to share the tip of the iceberg with you. Let me introduce you to the DISC Model of Human Behavior.

According to Dr. Rohm, the DISC Model of Human Behavior presents four main personality styles:

The **Dominant "D"** style is **outgoing** and **task-oriented**.

"Outgoing" means they operate by *taking action*.

"Task-oriented" means that they are highly focused on *getting things done*.

The **Inspiring "I"** style is **outgoing** and **people-oriented**.

"Outgoing" means they operate by *getting involved* and *being active*.

"People-oriented" means that they are highly focused on *people* and *relationships*.

The **Supportive "S"** style is **reserved** and **people-oriented**.

"Reserved" means they *prefer being in a relaxed environment* and *interacting one-on-one*.

"People-oriented" means that they are *in tune with people* and *relationships*.

The **Cautious "C"** style is **reserved** and **task-oriented**.

"Reserved" means they like to *take plenty of time to think things over*.

"Task-oriented" means that they are *focused on specific tasks*—even if the task is mental versus physical.

I will talk about the DISC Model of Human Behavior a bit more in Chapter 8 of this book.

CHAPTER 5

Opening your own driving school

I never have it in mind to start my own driving school. I knew it would take some time: apply, get the license and advertise to obtain customers. When I was in business school, I learned that you need to have enough cash on hand to be able to survive for two years while you get your business going.

My reality was that I was living from paycheck to paycheck. I had no savings. I had returned to university and just completed my Bachelor's of Education with a specialization in business and French. I have been married since 1993, and my wife and I had three young children, three boys. Plus, my late mother was living with us at that time. We had a mortgage to pay, plus utilities, food, two car payments and two car insurance payments as well.

Upon earning my teaching degree, I was hired as a full-time teacher in a different town to teach French as a second language, English in Grade 6 and home economics. I felt the job was a perfect match for me because of my background. Firstly, I was educated in the French language all my life. Secondly, I had received university training in fashion merchandising, and along the years I was trained in men's and women's pattern making.

Gaining employment in another town meant we had to move. So, I rented a place and move we did. Our home was on the market but it didn't sell. The teacher's salary was fine, however. But with my family to support and all the payments that would eventually become due each month I needed some extra money. The plan was to train students how to drive after they finished school for the day. My former employer gave me the info I needed in order to apply, plus I received some extra information from the government, so I applied for my driver training school license.

Six months later my official driver training school license arrived in the mail. It granted me the opportunity to officially operate a class 5 driver training program, which includes in-car lessons as well as classroom lessons. (Class 5 means passenger vehicles only.)

When you are operating a driver training school, you are, in fact, operating a business. Therefore, you are responsible for sales, promotion, marketing, setting up schedules for students and receiving payments from parents and students. It is nothing like going to work for a regular school or a company and having your paycheck deposited in your bank account hassle-free at the end of the month. In regular employment, you show up, you work, you socialize, you enjoy the benefits offered and you get paid the same amount month after month.

Conversely, when you operate your own business, it's like going hunting. You only eat what you kill. In other words, you are working only when you are face-to-face with students in the driver training classroom, or providing in-car lessons. Anything else you do—like calling and answering the phone, driving to pick up students, collecting money from customers, scheduling or cancelling driving sessions—all of those are warm-up activities. You don't get paid for that. As they say in golf: "You drive for show and you putt for dough."

Running your own business has its rewards, its advantages and its disadvantages. If you are in a relationship, or if you have a family— that means having a spouse and children involved—it will take a toll on them. If you operate in the town or city where you live and there is enough work, you can be home every day and adjust your schedule to suit family obligations like doctor's visits, travel, conferences and so on.

In my case, I had my family—my wife, three children and my late mother. I served towns that were far away from my home. Most of the time I was not able to go home every day. I used to be away 80% of the time during the week. There was very little to no work close to home. It was tough, to say the least, when I started the business full time. I would be away Mondays and Tuesdays, then home on Wednesdays, gone for Thursdays and Fridays and back home for the weekend. When we started to get more customers away from our area, I included Sundays on my work schedule as well. So, it was quite a challenge to balance work life and family life, especially when the bills were coming due and we needed a roof over our heads. But if my family needed me, I could rearrange my schedule and be available without a manager's approval.

There was no way I could come home when I had to work on a reserve or a settlement, they were just too far away. I stayed at hotels and got the work done as fast as I could. When my youngest child was on vacation or days-off, he and my wife came along with me, just to visit the places I was working in—mostly for the nice hotel stays and the food.

The cities or the communities you serve will determine whether you will be away or at home every night. The choice will be yours. I had no money to begin with, so I went where I was needed in order to earn the money to take care of my family. If I had to do it over again, I would not change anything because of all the lessons I have learned along the way.

Serving others gives me a lot of pleasure. I feel like I was born to serve and I do so gladly. For me, service comes first and money is secondary. As a matter of fact, whenever you put yourself in service, the money will follow. Or at least, it always did for me.

PURPOSE OF YOUR DRIVING SCHOOL BUSINESS

The management consultant Peter Drucker defines the purpose of a business as, "to create and keep a customer." The cost of creating a customer is very high. The cost of keeping them is extremely low.

HOW DO YOU GET TO KEEP YOUR CUSTOMERS?

It all has to do with the way you serve them the first time they deal with you. How well and how fast did you serve them?

According to Brian Tracy, one way to find out how happy your customers are is by asking them the magic question: "On a scale of 1 to 10, how would you rate our service to you?" Any answer that is not a 10 should be followed by this one: "What would it take for us to get a 10 from you the next time we serve you?"

The two most important words are "next time." You want to do business with them again next time. I have seen this principle being violated time and time again by my fellow driving instructors. If we don't serve our customers well enough, the most we can hope for is basic survival. When we make our customers happy, they come back to us and they recommend us to their friends.

Through one of his training seminars, I have heard Brian Tracy mention: "If you listen to your customers, they will make you rich." Listen to your customers. Work hard to amaze them to get that

10, which is the mark of excellence in service and, sure enough, their friends will be among your customers.

HOW DIFFERENT IS THE DRIVING SCHOOL BUSINESS?

A driving school business is different from any other business. You don't have to create the need, since it is already there. Your main job will be to convince your customers how better off they will be after using your services.

TELLING ISN'T SELLING

Most of the time, potential customers will call you for information. You are not there to give information, you are there to sell your services to them. Always ask for the order during your presentation, at the end of your presentation or at the moment that your customers give you a buying signal like: "How do I pay for it?" At that moment, they have made the decision to buy and you can stop selling.

METHODS OF PAYMENT

In the case of our school, potential buyers can stop by our place and pay for the services directly. They can also mail us a check or send an electronic transfer via their bank account. Some other driving schools are set up for credit cards as well.

Personally, I love when customers send their electronic transfer from the comfort of their homes. When I receive the email confirmation, I just go online and claim their payment.

Not all consumers are computer savvy. Some prefer the conventional ways of paying. And lots of foreigners prefer to pay us in cash for the driver training services. Either way, make sure you get paid, either partial or full payment. There is nothing worse than providing services to customers and then having to chase them to get paid. And lack of cash flow could be disastrous for your business.

CHAPTER 6

Recruiting other driving instructors

PROS AND CONS OF HIRING EMPLOYEES

Very few driving schools hire employees because they have difficulty in guaranteeing a certain number of working hours. Unless the school has been in business for a long time and the school is well established with a constant flow of customers, the school can't afford to hire employees as driving instructors.

When you hire an employee there are extra costs involved, like providing a car with driver training endorsement to that employee. All maintenance costs will have to be covered by the driving school. Remember, there will be also be social security benefits, employment insurance and worker's compensation insurance to pay for that employee.

HIRING CONTRACTORS

These contractors must already be licensed driving instructors. Most schools love going that route, because that will save a lot of money. Such contractors provide their own vehicle, car insurance and so on. And you are not responsible for any car maintenance costs, either.

Driving contractors have to pay their own taxes and for their own worker's compensation package. Work is offered to them on an as-needed basis. And you do not have to deal with any potential legal problems that may arise from firings or layoffs.

HIRING TEMPORARY FOREIGN WORKERS

To my knowledge, there are very few schools that hire temporary workers. You would need to recruit them from overseas and help them secure a work visa to be able to enter the country and work.

When they get here, they would have to speak English fluently, know how to drive very well and be able to meet provincial standards to obtain their instructor's license.

Before you dive into this kind of adventure, make sure you talk to Alberta Transportation (or your own province or state of residence) regarding licensing a temporary foreign worker.

Also, make sure you perform due diligence, because it could be difficult for you to know they are who they say they are. It may be virtually impossible to verify their driving abilities. Some workers may have no intention of working with you or for you. They might just be looking for a ticket to this land of opportunity. Make sure you are not taken for a ride.

HIRING NON-ALBERTA LICENSED DRIVING INSTRUCTORS

If they are already licensed by another province you may be able to help them secure their Alberta driving instructor's license. For more up-to-date information, please visit the Alberta Transportation website and find out what you need to do.

If they have never held an instructor's license before, they would have to satisfy all requirements set up by the government.

It is imperative that every instructor providing driver training for a fee in Alberta holds an instructor's license. Doing so without a proper license is illegal.

HIRING THE RIGHT INSTRUCTOR

Hiring the right instructor for your driving school is a very difficult endeavor. The fact that someone has an instructor's license does not necessarily mean that they will be a good fit for your driving school.

A great instructor should be:

- A team player.
- A very hard worker.

- An honest individual.

- Customer service-oriented.

- Someone who loves people with a desire to help them.

I have met a lot of instructors who only care about making money. They do not love people. They will only serve others when there is a profit to be made. If you make a mistake and hire such an instructor, it won't take long before they reveal to you who they really are.

You will know who they are when they collect money for services, chances are they will not hand that money to you. The late Zig Ziglar used to claim that he did not know someone until he did business with them. And Oprah Winfrey said: "Believe them the first time they show you who they are."

I'll add that once they show you that they are untrustworthy, get rid of them as fast as you can. You will do yourself a great favor. If you do not get rid of them it will not take long before they take even more advantage of you, and take you for a ride.

WHAT CAN YOU DO TO HIRE THE BEST?

I definitely recommend that you become knowledgeable about the DISC Model of Human Behavior, which will teach you about personality assessment and give you insight into the strengths and weaknesses of the individuals you intend to hire. Understand that by weaknesses, I'm referring to potential blind spots that those individuals might need to be aware of.

As the saying goes: "Your strengths will propel you, but your weaknesses should concern you." The great thing about DISC is that it is easy to understand and it can help you cover all the bases by hiring the right individual for the right position.

For any of you out there committed to learning more about the DISC model of human behavior, we offer DISC training through our company, *Learn 2 Change: A Leadership and Personal Development Company.*

At the time of the writing of this book, you can reach us at:

> Learn 2 Change
> 4903 – 47 St, Box 395
> Mirror, AB, T0B 3C0, Canada
>
> You can call us at: 780-806-9289 or 780-646-0055 or you can email us at: 1learn2change@gmail.com

CAN YOU PLACE RESTRICTIONS ON A DRIVING INSTRUCTOR?

Personally, I have never placed restrictions on any driving instructors. I let them know the nature of the driving school business. I have given them as much work as I can in the towns I work in. I let them know when I think work is going to be slow and that they should save for the rainy days.

Some driving instructors already operate their own driving school. Therefore, I share extra work with them. This becomes an issue when I expect them to serve my customers but they are actually serving their own customers without letting me know. When I hear my customers complaining about the instructors not showing up for a week or two, I take over immediately in order to satisfy the needs of my customers. And the relationship with those instructors peacefully ends.

Some other driving schools operate differently than we do. When you are in their employment, you are not allowed to accept work from any other driving school. What should you do when they have no work for you for an extended period of time while the school owner is working and making some money?

That was the case with one instructor who joined our school. He got a driving contract from another gentleman who was not good to do business with. So, I mentioned to my fellow instructor that, in Alberta, he was free to offer his services wherever he wanted. Plus, this instructor had his own school license as well. He just had a lot to learn.

I shared some work with the instructor for about six weeks to help him get on his feet. Then I passed him a contract that another driving school offered us. I did that for him because I strongly believe that I live in a land of abundance. Once you know you live in that kind of land, you realize you have so much to share and so much to give.

DELEGATION

You can't do everything by yourself, and you can't be in all places at all times. I just love it when Dr. Phil McGraw says: "You need a team." I knew it all along. When you start something from scratch and you have barely any money, it takes some time to set up a team. So, you need to delegate and let other instructors do more things for you in order to allow you to leverage your time.

RATE OF PAY

In the beginning, you should recruit instructors to do in-car lessons for you. You provide the students and they provide the driving lessons. In our driving school, we pay our instructors 75% of the fee we charge to our students. That may seem like a lot to someone who is not familiar with driver training, but this is not an 8 hour per day job. We operate in rural Alberta, an instructor may have to travel one to two hours before picking up their first students for the day and they don't get paid for travel time. They only get paid if and when they work. And if they don't work, they don't get paid. Therefore, this profession is not for everyone.

WHEN TO DELEGATE CLASSROOM INSTRUCTION TO AN INSTRUCTOR

You can also let an instructor do classroom instruction for you, but you have to be careful when considering this. You've got to choose the right person to help you. Personally, I would make sure the instructor has already served the school for many years.

With some instructors, after you have trained them to provide classroom instruction, you lose them within the following two years, or after they receive their driving school license. And, soon enough, they start to compete with you.

Loyalty is not the name of the game with these types of people. Once they become your competitor, they will wish that you no longer exist, and the best you can hope for is survival. They will do everything to cut the grass under your feet. It has happened to me and I have seen it happen to other driving schools as well.

I used to consider them as competitors, too, until I read Elbert Hubbard's advice in a book: "Do your work with all your heart and you will succeed. There is so little competition."

Despite everything the so-called competition has been doing to corner the whole market, I am still running around and doing business. When you serve a huge geographical area, "one" is too small a number to accomplish great things.

And to thrive in the world of driver training you have to do the following:

- Be both a very smart and a very hard worker.

- Make sure driver training is something you love to do and are passionate about.

- Make sure you always exceed all government expectations, because there is so little traffic once you go the extra mile.

- Attend conferences and seminars whenever you can, because only the cream of the cream does that. As we all know, "The cream always rises to the top."

- Deliver an "extra mile" level of service to your customers by always providing more. They will, in turn, reward you for it.

- Be patient, because one day they will come after you, instead of you having to chase after them.

And when that is done, you will know that you have become a highly effective driving instructor.

CHAPTER 7

Dancing with the competition

The Merriam-Webster dictionary defines competition as "the effort of two or more parties acting independently to secure the business of a third party by offering the most favorable terms."

When I started the driving school, I did not see myself as being in competition with another driving school. I was first looking to create my own job, because six people—including me—were dependent on my work to stay alive. A year or so later, when I got so much work that it was scattered throughout a wide geographical area, I could hire other instructors who needed jobs.

In this section of the book, you will learn about the following:

1. Why you should dance with the competition.

2. The kinds of competition you can dance with.

3. The kinds of competition you should not dance with.

4. Directing business to your competitors.

5. Learning from your competitors.

WHY YOU SHOULD DANCE WITH THE COMPETITION

When you first start operating your driving school, you basically have no customers yet. You do whatever you can to get some customers, starting with advertising. There will be very few driving schools willing to offer you customers to train for them. They might be afraid you will take away some of their market share. If, by any chance, they do offer you some work, I give you this advice: they are being good to you, therefore, be loyal to them.

I offered work to some fellow instructors who had just gotten their driving school license. It never occurred to me that they would end up competing with me in the future. I have always had an "abundance mindset." I don't mind sharing, because of abundance.

Once those instructors got enough money, all they do was to lower their prices in order to cut the grass under my feet. And they did. I lost market share in the rural areas I was operating in. But I do not hold grudges against anyone. I trained students in those areas when I could. I also travelled to other areas where no one else would go.

I still earned money, but in a different market area. To their surprise, every two years I buy a brand-new car, while my competitors still drive around with their old vehicles for about four years. I am sure they wonder how in the world I could get so much business for myself.

Hopefully they will learn about some of it in this book, and apply the same concepts that I used. One thing is for certain, I was born to serve, and every day that I wake up I have one question in mind: "Lord, whom can I serve today?"

I was created on purpose and for a purpose. I live that purpose every single day of my life. And I guarantee you, no one can duplicate that. There was no one like me before I got here, there are none like me while I am here and there won't be anyone like me when I depart. Isn't that wonderful to know?

When customers cancel their driving lesson, I am not frustrated. Brian Tracy put it this way: "It's God's gift of time." And I used that time to write the book that you are reading now. Isn't it great?

Again, when I started, I got some work from a College, which was a non-profit organization. At that time, their instructor quit and they called me to finish the job for them. Later on, I learned that the instructor did not enjoy working with a particular ethnic group. She insulted her students all the time. I never met that particular instructor, but I can promise you that she was not a people-oriented person. When you are not purposed to do something, you will frustrate yourself and you will frustrate the people you are working with.

I spent about three years, on and off, getting contracts from them until they hired their own instructor and I moved on. Three years later their instructor quit and they again called me to help out. I enjoyed teaching and I enjoyed driving. Being able to combine both is a great privilege for me. And when some managers say: "Wow, you guys are rewarded handsomely," I reply: "Why don't you give up your position and come do what we are doing?"

Lots of people do not want to go through what we go through, but they do want the rewards we receive without having to pay the price. Again, be loyal to everyone. They will always call you to help them when they need you. Be especially loyal to your customers, they are the reason you have a business. Exceed their expectations and your success is guaranteed. There are not many people out there committed to offering that "extra mile" level of service. This is the hallmark of the high achiever. And that's who you are: the highly effective driving instructor.

THE KINDS OF COMPETITION YOU CAN DANCE WITH

Colleges – A College, or a school operating as a not-for-profit organization are your best bets. They get the contracts, then they give you a piece of them. If you do the work they will always pay you. Cooperate with these bureaucrats, they love shuffling papers. Do not give them any trouble, otherwise your check will always be late. I treat these office employees well. I send my invoice before it's due and I call them to make sure they check their email. If your invoice is late, you can forget about getting paid on time. I follow up until they tell me my check is in the mail, and if I don't see it within one week, I call again. Remember to always be nice. It really pays off.

A failing driving school – When they get in contact with you, you'll know it. They have no money and they max out their credit cards trying to survive. When I had too many contracts to handle on my own, I would just pass the extras on to someone in dire need. I don't want customers to have to wait for me for three weeks or more, especially those who are very time-conscious or impatient, the type that when they want something, they want it last week. And you have to know how to spot those customers.

Once you collect their money they cannot wait to be served. They booked their road test before they even talked to you, and they demand that you move everybody aside for them so they can be at the front of the line. These are the most difficult customers you will ever have to deal with.

OUTSOURCING THE CLASSROOM PORTION

To my knowledge, at this time in Alberta we have two driving schools that offer the classroom portion of driver training online: *AMA Driver Education* and *A Driving School* (managed by Fleet Safety International in Calgary, AB). Alberta Transportation allows them to offer these online sessions. I deal with both of them and saved a tremendous amount of time. My students no longer have to wait for me to set up a live classroom for them.

As I mentioned before, I work mostly in rural Alberta. Therefore, I am a moving target. I travel from town to town so I can keep busy. When students come to me on a one-to-one basis, I refer them to the online schools for classroom sessions. When I have six or more students I teach them face-to-face. It works out best for all of us.

On a side note, I would like to thank some fellow instructors whom I used to give work to for their fierce competition. Because of it, I have found ways to grow myself through seminars and conferences, and therefore, I am now qualified to provide training in the personal development field. Also, when work was slow, I used that time to write books such as the one you are reading now, and there are many more I am working on during my free time. Without them as my teachers I would not have been able to even think about creating multiple sources of income for myself. Once again, I thank them for acting the way they did and for being who they are. They helped me to embark on a different path of enlightenment.

Today, I am happy to quote: "Amateurs compete. Professionals create."

Look for those professionals out there who will not see you as competitors. You are not out there to win and to make them lose. You want to bake a bigger cake together so there will be larger pieces that neither of us could create alone. Dr. Steven Covey named this principle "synergize." And that is really one of the principles that all highly effective people live by. They are either looking for a win-win situation or for no deal at all. In the end, there is no better way to live or to do business.

THE KINDS OF COMPETITION YOU SHOULD NOT DANCE WITH

You should definitely not do business with someone who engages in a win-lose situation with you. In other words, they will win and you will lose. They probably won't give you any customers to train for them. If they do, make sure they pay you for your services first, and then you should treat the customers you are working with like royalty. I promise these happy customers will refer more of their friends back to you. And if you do not trust a driving school owner you should not do business with that person at all.

DIRECTING BUSINESS TO YOUR COMPETITORS

It is entirely up to you whether or not you want to send business to your competitors. I personally believe that if I am destined to drive with someone, then I will indeed drive with that person. That stems from my religious upbringing. I love saying: "I will have everything that has my name on it." With that kind of attitude, I feel calm and I am at peace.

Also, with my "abundance" mindset, I strongly believe there is more than enough to go around in this world. I used to direct business to a fellow instructor who created his job just like I did. I could see the joy in his face when he got more work than I did in a particular area. In fact, he charged 40% less than I did. You know, in this life, you cannot hide who you are for long. To make a long story short, he disappeared and went far away to places from where he is not able to get back home every night. I again got calls in that area and I got more business. "Slow and steady wins the race." I am not only in another kind of race, but I'm in that race all by myself.

Sometimes when I get a call from a potential customer, I already have lots of work and there is no way I can get to them. I know another instructor who is not busy, so I give the caller the other instructor's number. I have done this for years for that same instructor. But he has never dialed my number or sent me a text or an email to thank me for referring business to him. I am certainly not complaining. I am just living by the words of the late Dr. Wayne Dyer: "Do good to them even if a thank you is not forthcoming. Your good gesture is never between you and them. It is between you and your Creator."

On the same line of thought, Mother Teresa said:

"The good you do today will be forgotten. Do good anyway.

Give the best you have and it will never be enough. Give your best anyway."

You should live your life like that. And you will be rewarded for it.

Once you are a servant, or you adopt the attitude of a servant, you will always have some work because the world has so many people that you can serve. Share with them. There is plenty to go around.

It is my understanding that we came into this world empty-handed and we will depart from it empty-handed as well. The best we can do is to love and to share.

LEARNING FROM YOUR COMPETITORS

This quote is worth repeating: "Do your work with all your heart. There is so little competition."

From what little competition there is out there, you can learn:

What makes customers go to them?

Is it a lower price? If it is, don't even bother matching it. You are providing a service. Make sure you offer a high-quality service with fast delivery. After all, any instructor can replicate capital. High quality service is hard to beat.

Let them keep driving around with their low prices. Remember, the fees for servicing your driver-training vehicle will not go down at the dealership or at a mechanical service shop. Tires and parts for your vehicle always go up in value. You'll see how long they will be able to keep their fees low.

I mentioned earlier that I purchase a brand-new car every two years. Most of the time, I either pay half up front or write a check for the whole amount to the dealership, and then I drive away with my car. With a brand-new car I have peace of mind on the road at all times.

I am not saying this to impress anyone. I just want to impress upon you that if you love what you do and you do it with all your heart, you will become a master at what you are doing. There are a lot of customers out there with cash in their hands ready to pay you to serve them.

How reliable is your competitor to their customers?

You are reliable only to the degree that people can count on you to do what you promise you will do. But if you are sick, or your car breaks down, they will understand.

In the beginning, it was never about competition for me, and to this very day I still do not see myself as competing with anybody.

I do my work with all my heart and I let the public decide if they would like to work with me or not. I also consider myself a missionary wherever I provide my driver training services. I will know when my time is up, and I will let everyone else know about it as well. I do not have an eternal contract on this Earth. While I am still here, I shall travel around and serve.

How well you treat a fellow instructor?

Remember that a fellow instructor is a human "being" and not a human "doing." You need to treat your instructors well in every way. Your instructors' strengths are your business' greatest assets.

Ask yourself this question: "How would you like to be treated if the roles were reversed?" There may be a better rule than the golden rule, but no one has found it yet. In the meantime: "Do unto others as you would like them to do unto you."

Take the high road – I know how I was treated when I started to work as a driving instructor so that I could feed my family. I got very little work, while the people working for the school with seniority got all of it. I did not complain. I used all that free time to attend university classes, and at the end I obtained my Bachelor of Education degree.

I also know how fellow instructors treated me when they obtained their driving school license. Some just stopped serving our customers and never let me know. That was very unprofessional, to say the least. I had customer complaints, but I overcame this difficulty by offering extra driving time to our students who were not served well.

When I called my instructors to help, it was one excuse after another, like: "I had to go hunting to get meat for the winter," or, "My child was sick." In Canada, we have different ways of communicating. They could call me, text me, email me or send me a message on Facebook. But they used none of these media to let me know. In summary, they just dropped me once they were legally able to operate on their own.

You could tell that gratitude was never a part of their vocabulary. I gave them work, I paid them well, but their way of thanking me was to hand over a whole bunch of irate customers to deal with. Of course, I took responsibility for what had happened because I was the one who hired those instructors.

I did learn a lot by being exposed to that kind of behavior. I came out stronger than before. I concluded that I was in the presence of instructors with a "scarcity mindset," even if they were born right here in Canada and still live here.

However, there are some great instructors out there, too. You will meet them during your career. Once you do, hire them and always treat them well. And always take the high road; treat others better than they treated you.

Is the competition returning calls to their customers?

One thing you should know for sure, customers do not call you to entertain themselves. Do not assume they have nothing to do. Your potential customers call you to put money in your pocket, so treat them like royalty. Call them right back. In our driving school, we do our best to call them back immediately. If our customers feel they got a late call-back, it is because we could not reach them the first time, likely their voice mail was full so we could not leave a message for them.

Text message – It is a lot more convenient to send a text message back to our customers. If we cannot reach them by phone we send a text to the phone number they called us from.

A year or so ago, the telephone company sent us a reply telling us that our message was delivered to a landline—a home phone. When that happened, we knew we had to call them again. But nowadays, we no longer get a reply from the telephone company telling us that we texted a home phone. We only know if we have reached our customer via a cell phone when they text us back.

Have someone handle your calls – You should definitely have someone to handle your calls for you. Pick that person carefully, because it could mean the difference between success and failure.

In our driving school, our customers can reach me on my cell phone or my wife on her cell phone. When a potential customer calls me while I am providing in-car instruction, I have that call forwarded to my wife, and she takes care of that customer. The message to her is as follows: "Please call this number NOW."

NOW means NOW; not later, not after a nap, not after cooking. When a customer calls, it is like royalty showing up to your door. Everything else can wait.

Customers bring cash and cash is the lifeblood of your business. If you don't believe it, ask the instructor who lives from paycheck to paycheck with no money in the bank, who panics and complains to you when work slows down. That instructor will tell you that it's not a great way to live. If you give priority to your customers and you SERVE them well, they will be happy. And happy customers refer you to their friends. And you, in turn, will be laughing all the way to the bank.

I mentioned this before and it is worth repeating again, from Brian Tracy: "If you listen to your customers, they will make you rich." When your customers call you, pick up the phone and listen to them. If you don't, you're going to have skinny kids.

CHAPTER 8

The Model of Human Behavior

Let me offer a brief review of the Model of Human Behavior:

According to Dr. Rohm, the DISC Model of Human Behavior presents four main personality styles:

The **Dominant "D"** style is **outgoing** and **task-oriented**.

"Outgoing" means they operate by *taking action*.

"Task-oriented" means that they are highly focused on *getting things done*.

The **Inspiring "I"** style is **outgoing** and **people-oriented.**

"Outgoing" means they operate by *getting involved* and *being active*.

"People-oriented" means that they are highly focused on *people* and *relationships*.

The **Supportive "S"** style is **reserved** and **people-oriented**.

"Reserved" means they *prefer being in a relaxed environment* and *interacting one-on-one*.

"People-oriented" means that they are *in tune with people* and *relationships*.

The **Cautious "C"** style is **reserved** and **task-oriented**.

"Reserved" means they like to *take plenty of time to think things over*.

"Task-oriented" means that they are *focused on specific tasks*—even if the task is mental versus physical.

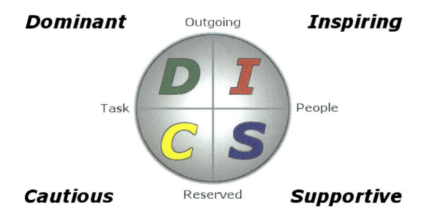

This time, make an educated guess of your personality style. Look at the descriptive DISC letters and ask:

- Are you outgoing or reserved?
- Are you task-oriented or people-oriented?

You are considered a:

- "D" type if you are outgoing and task-oriented.
- "I" type if you are outgoing and people-oriented.
- "S" type if you are reserved and people-oriented.
- "C" type if you are reserved and task-oriented.

You may be saying that you feel like you have a little bit of each in you. Yes, you do. No one is purely a D, I, S, or C, but rather we are all a blend of each of those four, to a greater or a lesser degree.

For an accurate picture of your personality style, you may consider taking a DISC personality assessment. Once you know your personality style, it is important to be able to quickly make an assessment about the type of student you are interacting with, so that you can adapt or adjust your personality style in order to become an effective driving instructor.

RECOGNIZING TELL-TALE TRAITS OF YOUR STUDENTS:

HOW TO RECOGNIZE A DOMINANT "D" STYLE STUDENT:

When a "D" student calls you on the phone and you do not answer, they will call you again and again. They prefer talking instead of texting. If you do answer the call, you will probably hear: "Where are you?"

When a "D" student agrees to drive with you, he/she expects you to be on time. If you are not, even one to two minutes before the agreed-on time, your phone will ring. And when you meet them, the unhappiness will show on their face. They will not greet you, they will not talk to you. They will not even shake your hand, because you were late. They take lateness as a personal insult to them.

On the other hand, when a "D" student is late, they expect you to wait for them. They want you to be happy that they have shown up. In summary, they don't mind making you wait, but they hate waiting for you.

When a "D" student requests a driving session, either by phone or face-to-face, they expect you to give them the time they ask for. In other words, they want you to move your schedule around and give them the requested time.

Each time a "D" student shows up for a driving session, you can forget about socializing, instead, focus on driving right away.

When you drive with a "D" student, expect them not to obey the traffic regulations. For a "D," the rules are there for others, not for them. Expect them to speed whether the street is busy or not, or whether it is a school zone or a playground zone. They won't slow down, either, when turning right or left. A "D" style only knows two speeds: zero or full throttle.

By the way, I recommend that every instructor get at least a million-dollar life insurance policy to protect their family—especially if your family depends on you—in case something happens.

Read this post written on social media by a fellow driving instructor:

> Well, one week and one day until the nightmares of being a driving instructor are over!!! No more leaving my life in the hands of a 15-16-year-old!

After I read that post, I can absolutely conclude that this male driving instructor must have been in the presence of some "D" style students, and wasn't even aware of it.

HOW TO RECOGNIZE AN INSPIRING "I" STYLE STUDENT:

If a student shows up to the first driving session without their learner's license, I can promise you with 95 % accuracy that you are dealing with an "I" type. The beauty of this is that it does not matter what their race, color or ethnic background is. I have seen this behavior time and time again. Please remind your students via a phone call or a text to bring their learner's. Let them know they will be charged for the missed appointment if they show up without it, too. In the province of Alberta, a student driver must carry their learner's license with them every time they drive with you in the car. Failure to do so will result in a fine if you get stopped by a peace officer. Moreover, a driving instructor is not allowed to provide driving instruction if the student fails to show up for their lesson with their learner's.

Recognize that an "I" style moves fast. They love smiling and are people-oriented, so they enjoy talking. Remember to get them to focus on driving at all times while you are with them. Most of the talking you do during the lesson should be related to driving.

The more you talk to them, the more distracted they will be, and they will lose focus because they will be looking at you instead of the traffic ahead of, or around, the car.

Keep in mind that "I" types do not pay attention to details and can have short attention spans. So, pay more attention than usual while you are in their presence.

When an "I" style shows up to work with you, it is very easy to tell. They seem to be saying: "Look at me!" You may notice tattoos, hair styles that attract attention or fashionable shoes or clothes.

"I" types are high on enthusiasm. You may spot them by the way they interact with everybody around them. To them, a stranger is a friend they have not met yet. So, they make friends easily.

"I" types learn fast. You might have to keep them focused on the task at hand so they can learn the driving maneuvers you need to teach them. You can give them a high-five when they do something well, which will show them that you speak their language.

Expect to have lots of fun when you work with the Inspiring style. Keep track of the time, because they won't. They are just so happy to be with people. Expect them to be late for appointments, and go easy on them. "I" types are very forgiving if you are late for appointment for any reason, and they will be glad to see you when you show up.

HOW TO RECOGNIZE A SUPPORTIVE "S" STYLE STUDENT:

An "S" style student is people-oriented. As a driving instructor, they will be nice to you and they will expect you to be nice to them as well. You will enjoy teaching this type the most.

When you meet an "S," expect them to be reserved. "S" types will say hello and greet you warmly. As an individual, you matter more to them than the task at hand. When they show up to the lesson, take a minute to show them you care by asking questions about them and their family.

Let them know about the maneuvers you expect them to learn or practice that day and avoid surprising them. They don't like surprises. Give them a heads-up about where you will take them. You might have to show confidence in them when it is time to go onto a busy street or a highway.

Pay attention when the "S" style is talking to you and do not interrupt. What they say is not necessarily what they mean. For example, if an "S" student asks you if you want to go to the bathroom, they are telling you that they want to go to the bathroom. So, if you do not then look for a restaurant, or another place where they can use the bathroom, you are not speaking their language. You both may be speaking English, but you'd be missing the mark. Then when you volunteer to stop, you will show them that you are sensitive to their needs. They will be happy with you and they will recommend you to their friends.

An "S" type does not mind doing routine work. Therefore, make them practice the driving maneuvers many times until they know how to do them. Take the time to demonstrate the maneuvers first before you ask them to practice.

You should not scream or yell at an "S" style. They may not come back to you again. (A "D" style instructor with little patience might be tempted to yell during instruction.)

Your voice should definitely be used in low tones for an "S" individual. Pay attention to what they are saying to you.

"S" types wear clothes for comfort. So look for light blue or conservative colors. They will not wear anything that attracts attention to them.

HOW TO RECOGNIZE A CAUTIOUS "C" STYLE STUDENT:

If you show up to an appointment ten minutes or more before the agreed-upon time and your student is already there, chances are you are dealing with a "C" style student. And therefore, don't expect to be greeted warmly, because the "C" is reserved and task-oriented.

When a "C" sits down behind the wheel, expect them to look around and notice everything, because they pay a lot of attention to details. Make sure your vehicle is always clean and not cluttered. Keep all unwanted stuff in the trunk of your car.

Again, a "C" style has his/her mind set up on task. Some of them do need to work on their people skills, so they do not like small talk. They think it is a waste of time.

In terms of learning, expect "C" types to be able to quickly learn and master what you teach them in the vehicle. This is the type that school is made for, the rest of us just adapt to it. Model the driving maneuvers for them, and the "C" style will enjoy learning from you.

Make sure you provide clear and accurate explanation to a "C" style student. Don't correct them when they talk because they take it very personally and can hold grudges for a long time.

"C" types tend to be clean, and if your car isn't, don't expect them not to notice. You might feel embarrassed if they mention it. They will feel very uncomfortable if your car is dirty and cluttered, it is a personal insult to them.

You need to know that "C" types are very hard on themselves, and on others. If they are late, don't even mention it. They have already punished themselves mentally.

"C" types probably won't stop for a bathroom break. They pay you to drive with them, not for you to go use the washroom on their time. If you do use a washroom, know that the clock started to tick when you left. They are counting to see how long it will take you to get back.

Therefore, when you drive with a "C" style student, let them know that you will give them extra time, so there is no conflict between you. "C" types document everything. They will let you know how much time you owe them. So never argue, just give them their time back. They will trust you and they will send customers your way.

When you realize that a "C" student is ready for the road test, please let them know. They will think there is always room to master their skills. If a parent or someone else is paying, a "C" always requests extra driving time. If they have to pay you, they will go for their road test first. And I have never seen any of my "C" style students take their road test twice during my ten plus years of driver training in Alberta

CHAPTER 9

Interacting with students

"D" INSTRUCTOR WITH A "D" STUDENT:

You are both strong-minded individuals and you both love to be in control. As an instructor, you are legally in charge when the student is in your car. Be flexible and let them have some control.

"D" INSTRUCTOR WITH AN "I" STUDENT:

Let them talk and tell some jokes or stories. But remember to stay focused on the road, since your student might not pay too much attention to their driving. They might be looking at you while talking to you.

"D" INSTRUCTOR WITH AN "S" STUDENT:

Slow down when you talk to an "S" and be friendly. Do not interrupt when they talk to you. Teach them one driving maneuver at a time. Let them practice more so they can build confidence in themselves while learning how to drive.

"D" INSTRUCTOR WITH A "C" STUDENT:

Provide clear and accurate instruction to a Cautious style individual. When they ask you a question, a "C" expects quality answers. When you ask them a question, give them time to think, and let them practice as much as they can. A "C" loves learning, and driving is no different.

"I" INSTRUCTOR WITH A "D" STUDENT:

Do not waste time. Get down to business and let your student drive as soon as you meet them. Forget your jokes and small talk. A "D" is task-oriented. Get to the task, be good and they will love you.

"I" INSTRUCTOR WITH AN "I" STUDENT:

You are both people-oriented. Remember, you are here to work, not to visit or socialize. You are not there to plan a party. Focus on the work at hand and be careful. Driving instruction is a serious business.

"I" INSTRUCTOR WITH AN "S" STUDENT:

You are both people-oriented. So do not try to be over-friendly by talking too much. Remember to focus on driving and teach them the driving techniques they pay you for. Remember: "Labor is more important than oratory."

"I" INSTRUCTOR WITH A "C" STUDENT:

You enjoy talking, but a "C" does not like to talk much. Cut the stories and don't be silly. Provide clear and accurate instruction and stick to the task at hand. Remember that a "C" documents everything. If you waste time, your manager will find out.

"S" INSTRUCTOR WITH A "D" STUDENT:

Remember that a "D" student will want to be in control. If you let that happen, you will regret it. As an instructor, you are legally in charge when a student is in your car. So, take charge and remind them they are not. Threaten to stop their instruction and if you have to, or refer them to another driving instructor.

"S" INSTRUCTOR WITH AN "I" STUDENT:

Remember to focus on the task at hand and do not let the "I" type ramble. They enjoy telling jokes. Safety is the most important concern in providing driving instruction.

"S" INSTRUCTOR WITH AN "S" STUDENT:

You are both cut from the same cloth. You will get along very well during your time together. You need to be more confident. You may have to push your "S" student in order to get better driving results.

"S" INSTRUCTOR WITH A "C" STUDENT:

You are people-oriented, therefore customer-service oriented. Your "C" student is a task-oriented individual. Focus on the task at hand and be ready to enjoy some quiet moment in the car. You can certainly talk to your "C" student. When you do, bear in mind that they may tune you out. Don't take it personally.

"C" INSTRUCTOR WITH A "D" STUDENT:

Be brief and direct when working with a "D" student. Do not overwhelm them with detailed explanations. As a "C" instructor, your tendency is to stay below the speed limit or to conform to traffic regulations. Expect a "D" student to disregard the rules of the road. To a "D," the regulations are for others. The potential for conflict is high between the two of you if you do not understand each other.

"C" INSTRUCTOR WITH AN "I" STUDENT:

Loosen up a little bit and let them talk. Laugh at their jokes or stories. Never tell them that their jokes are not funny, they will take it personally. Do not give them detailed explanations. Do not expect them to be as detail-oriented as you are. In fact, they can be easily excited and distracted. During your time with them, they will bring some fun into your life.

"C" INSTRUCTOR WITH AN "S" STUDENT:

Both of you are reserved individuals. Your time together can be quiet and it will go smoothly. Let them practice so they can learn the driving techniques. Talk to them about family, since "S" types are family-oriented. And be friendly to them as well.

"C" INSTRUCTOR WITH A "C" STUDENT:

You will enjoy each other's company very much, because both of you speak the same language. You both obey traffic regulations. Your instruction will be followed as you expect it to be, because you are cut from the same cloth. Safety will definitely not be a concern since you will look out for each other.

For more knowledge on the DISC Model of Human Behavior, you may consider attending one of our trainings. You can get in touch with us by mail at:

Learn 2 Change
4903-47 St, Box 395,
Mirror, AB, T0B 3C0, AB
Canada

You can also reach us through our driver training school:

Saint Paul Driving School

5413 – 51 Ave

St. Paul, AB, T0A 3A3

Canada

Our telephone numbers: 780-646-0055 or 780-806-9289

Our email addresses: 1learn2change@gmail.com

or stpauldrivingschool@gmail.com

WORKING WITH PERSONALITY BLENDS

If you were to attend one of our trainings you would go through a personality assessment. From that assessment you would learn how to read your personality graphs. The first graph would be your Environmental style—how you believe you should behave in order to become successful in your environment. The second graph would be your Basic style—the way you behave most naturally when you are on autopilot.

In previous pages, I mentioned that you have a predominant trait. It can be "D," "I," "S" or "C." I also mentioned that each of us has every trait in us, to a greater or a lesser degree.

Keep in mind that your personality blend involves one predominant trait and one supportive trait above the midline on your personality graph. One example would be the Dominant Inspiring "D/I" type.

Your blend can also involve one predominant trait and two supportive traits above the midline of your personality graph. An example would be the Dominant Inspiring Supportive "D/I/S" type.

For the purpose of keeping this book short, I have chosen to only talk about three blends of each predominant trait. Here they are:

THE "D" WITH THE "I" BLEND:

The Dominant/Inspiring type is very active and action-oriented. As soon as they get into your car, get going and do not waste time. This type is also people-oriented. They are likely to share a lot of personal stories with you. Do not be surprised if they share their personal life as well.

The ones that I drove with changed jobs very often and left their parental home early, even before they graduated from high school. Once you are done teaching them the driving maneuvers, let them choose the streets they want to travel on and also when to practice their parking as well.

THE "D" WITH THE "S" BLEND:

The Dominant/Supportive type is called a "cross personality" blend. It could be very difficult to drive with a student who is wired this way.

At one point the student will want to be in charge. At another time, they will want to help and support you.

The ones I have driven with changed their pick-up location very often and expected me to adjust to them. However, they are enjoyable to teach because they are both task- and people-oriented. Be aware that they can switch from the "D" to the "S" and vice versa without warning. Your job is to know at every moment which of these styles the student is operating from.

THE "D" WITH THE "C" BLEND:

The Dominant/Cautious style is very task-oriented. They speak very little when they get into your car. They learn very fast. When I have to do five two-hour sessions with them, they will know all the driving maneuvers they have to learn by session number three. For our remaining time together, I let them drive around and practice their parking. You can let them drive on the highway but you have to be very careful. They travel fast. And if they are hockey players, they will drive even faster. Remember to get the life insurance we were talking about earlier for your loved ones, because you never know. Your loved ones might need it in case you are no longer able to provide for them.

THE "I" WITH THE "D" BLEND:

The Inspiring/Dominant style is very outgoing and enjoys being with people. You can talk to them while they drive, but be careful. They may get distracted and not stop for stop signs or red lights. So keep your talking related to driving most of the time. The Inspiring/Dominant style never runs out of things to say.

THE "I" WITH THE "S" BLEND:

The Inspiring/Supportive type enjoys being around people. Socialize a little with them and make them feel valuable. Keep their attention focused on driving. Practice the driving maneuvers repeatedly and allow them time to master them. Congratulate them when they accomplish a good maneuver or practice a technique well. They love attention.

THE "I" WITH THE "C" BLEND:

The Inspiring/Cautious type has two opposite sets of traits. They are outgoing, and also people-oriented. They want to have fun learning with you and they also want to make sure they perform their driving techniques perfectly. Give them opportunities to practice repeatedly with you. Always provide them with clear instructions. Cheer them up and do not talk down to them. And, lastly, keep all your appointments with them.

THE "S" WITH THE "D" BLEND:

As mentioned in the Dominant/Supportive style, the Supportive/ Dominant style also has a "cross personality" blend. They are people-oriented and also task-oriented. They will cooperate with you when you teach them. They may seem shy, but they can take initiative as well. Lower the tone of your voice when talking to them and do not interrupt when they talk. Provide them sufficient time to practice with you, and let them have a say in their learning. Also, be aware that they can switch from the "S" to the "D" and vice versa without warning. Your job is to know at every moment which style the student is operating from.

THE "S" WITH THE "I" BLEND:

The Supportive/Inspiring type is warm and friendly. They are the sweetest type you'll ever have to work with. They will cooperate with your instruction. Avoid being angry when working with them, and use a low tone of voice when instructing them. Show sincere appreciation in them. Model the driving maneuvers for them to execute, and provide enough practice time. Avoid criticizing them. They take it personally.

THE "S" WITH THE "C" BLEND:

The Supportive/Cautious style is very cautious in everything they do. Expect them to abide by the traffic rules. They will not take the risk of speeding. Because they are reserved, do not be angry when working with them, as they prefer a peaceful environment. Make sure they understood everything you say. Provide them with a schedule of their appointments with you and make sure you keep them, unless you have a car breakdown.

THE "C" WITH THE "D" BLEND:

The Cautious/Dominant style is highly task-oriented. The task is more important than people to them. Provide clear instructions when you work with them, and expect very little talk. Make sure you follow through on all the commitments you have with them and always be on time (preferably earlier than the scheduled time). They will take your lateness very personally. Your vehicle must be very clean and free from clutter. As a side note, this type is extremely difficult to please.

THE "C" WITH THE "I" BLEND:

The Cautious/Inspiring style is cautious by nature. This style is comprised of two sets of opposite traits. Provide clear instructions, and allow no room for misunderstanding. Provide recognition for every maneuver they execute well. They may lean on you for a lot of help, so help them as required. As a highly effective driving instructor, they expect you to be up to par.

THE "C" WITH THE "S" BLEND:

The Cautious/Supportive style is reserved and careful. Use reassuring voice tones to show that you are sincere and appreciative of their company. Let them know the driving maneuver you are about to practice with them before you begin. They may look like they are not confident, but rest assured they can get the job done. Do not hurry when they ask you questions, and provide quality answers. When they are ready for their road test, let them know it, even if they think otherwise. Loan them your confidence and you will not be disappointed.

CHAPTER 10

Dealing with potential customers

WHAT KIND OF CUSTOMERS ARE YOU DEALING WITH?

Now that you are familiar with the Model of Human Behavior, you can make an educated guess of the type of customers you are dealing with, on the phone or in person.

On the phone, you are going to have to rely on their tone of voice, and how fast or slow they may be talking. It will be easier when they are face-to-face with you. You can rely on their facial expressions, body language or gestures.

When customers text you, you also need to pay attention to the words they use to communicate with you.

In any case, you need to do your best to pinpoint that person's personality style so you can interact with them accordingly. To communicate back to them, ask yourself what a Supportive type would do. "S" types would be nice to the customers, and they would serve them with the utmost respect. Remember that customers are there for you to serve them and when you do, they bring you money.

DEALING WITH SOMEONE BORN IN CANADA:

Since we are located in English Canada, the people we deal with already speak English. You'll be speaking English with them when presenting or selling your services. They could be people with parents originating from other countries. If so, that could influence the way you interact with each other. In that case, be culturally aware of what their upbringing could bring into the relationship.

DEALING WITH FIRST NATIONS STUDENTS:

Up until the date of writing this book, I have worked on eleven different First Nations reserves in Alberta. I started helping them back in 2009 and now we are in 2018. The cultures are pretty much the same, but individuals act differently from one reserve to the next.

I enjoy working with First Nations. I am so excited when they pass their road test and receive their driver's license. They can finally drive legally on the road, get a wonderful job and change their life and the lives of those around them.

Treat them with care and help them learn how to drive. When I work off-reserve I wear a tie, so when I work on-reserve, I also wear a tie. In other words, I dress up every day. I pick them up from their training centers, from the band offices or sometimes from their homes when they cannot get a ride to meet me. Sometimes I get lost because the home is located seven to ten kilometers from the main road, so I will call them so they can guide me (I probably missed a turn). They love being helped, and lots of them have become my friends.

DEALING WITH IMMIGRANTS FROM OTHER COUNTRIES:

When you teach students how to drive, they will come from different countries. Because of that, English is our common language of communication, and that presents some issues. Some immigrants are easier to understand than others because of their accents. Be careful, slow down and make sure they understand.

Some immigrants complain that the fee is expensive compared to their countries of origin. "Why didn't you learn how to drive before coming here?" I always replied, to which I received all kinds of answers. Which is more expensive: paying the fee or walking around when it is -32 degrees Celsius?

They also convert the fee they pay in their mind with regards to the Canadian equivalent in their country. It is good to remind them of the same thing the customs agents told us when we came to this country: "Welcome to Canada."

At the end of the day, they paid the fee and they drove. I rely on my immigrant friends. They keep me busy on the road and they help me take care of my family. And I am grateful for that. Thank you for making the trip to Canada.

DEALING WITH IMMIGRANT CHILDREN:

When these children call you, be ready to be on the phone for longer than you anticipated. They speak English when they request the information from you, but then they have to stop talking to you and translate it back to their parents who do not speak a lot of English.

Be nice and be patient. Pretty soon they will transfer money into your account. Those kids have to learn and they do not have a choice. Mom and Dad demanded it and they have to comply. Once they get the license, they are never at home. They are out enjoying their newly-acquired freedom behind the wheel. Help them get their driver's license and they will love you for it.

"I WILL THINK ABOUT IT."

According to Brian Tracy, when you hear this from a customer, it is   customer speak for "good bye." They are not ready to buy from you yet. That could be due to several reasons:

- ◆ No money, no sale.
- ◆ No urgency, no sale.
- ◆ No need, no sale.
- ◆ No authority, no sale.

"I'LL TALK TO MY SPOUSE OR MY CHILD."

The spouse or the child could be the decision maker. A Dominant "D" parent would not use that language. The Dominant parent would make the decision and the child would have to comply. In other words, the boss decides and the crew follows. I love "D" parents. The payment gets to your bank account fast and you earn the money fast. But be ready to move as fast as the "D" parents want you to move.

If the spouse or the child is of any other personality style, well, there is no rush. You have to be patient to get them to call you back. I wait for a day or two to either call them back myself or get my wife to call to press for a decision.

CHAPTER 11

Handling customer complaints

If you handle your contract quickly, no one is likely to complain. If they do, they will likely have a good reason. Always provide a driving schedule for them even if it is three or four weeks in the future. If you incur trouble with your car, let your customers know as quickly as possible, and they will understand. Always be truthful and get the car fixed as fast as possible.

Personally, I schedule a time every day for preventive maintenance. You could also schedule your maintenance at a time when the business isn't busy. When my car breaks down, it is always unexpected. I buy a brand new car every two years because we drive at least one hundred thousand kilometers per year. Therefore, the car has to be maintained so I get as little downtime as possible.

Another cause of complaints to us has to do with the fact that we outsource our classroom sessions to an online school. This has nothing to do with our online partner, however. Customers sometimes complain to us when they cannot get to their class file because they let their time expire. We will then ask them to call our online partner to help.

Some students are not proficient in computer skills and that can be a problem. Sometimes they might live on a farm and have a slow internet connection. Encourage them to go to their town library or school library to access the online training in their free time.

WHO IS MOST LIKELY TO COMPLAIN?

It all depends. If a Dominant type complains, get the problem solved fast. Most of them are very impatient because they have so much on their plate. Drop everything and get the issue solved. These folks live by one motto: "Do it now." Practice this and you will get so much accomplished in your life.

If an Inspiring type complains, you will know why. They have started their project but let it slide, but they will get back to it a few months later. These individuals are people-oriented. Keep them accountable by checking up on them and help them to do what they have to do. As a reminder, "I" types are great starters but tend to be poor finishers. Help them to finish as fast as they can.

A Supportive type client is not likely to complain. If they do, they will have a great reason for doing so. "S" types are people-oriented and they will cooperate with you. They are nice people, so be nice in return. Solve their issues and they will send customers your way.

A Cautious style individual will keep an account on you even if you are one minute late to pick them up, or if your car is dirty or cluttered. Make sure they are completely satisfied by keeping all promises made to them, because they document everything. They will respect you for it and trust you even more. Remember that happy customers will refer their friends to you.

CHAPTER 12

Dealing with the government

At the time of this writing, we operate in the province of Alberta, Canada. Here we deal with three levels of government:

LOCAL

They expect you to have a business license from each town or city you operate in, which you pay for every year. There is always a fee increase when you renew. If you work out of town, you get charged more. If you no longer operate in a place because of lack of business you should let the municipal office know, otherwise they will send you a bill. If you go in the middle of the year to pay the license fee, they will charge you the full amount regardless of how many months you are going to work in that town.

PROVINCIAL

On the provincial level, we deal with Alberta Transportation for our driving school license, which you have to renew every year. The instructors have to renew their instructor's licenses every two years. Cooperate with those government officials and you will have smooth sailing. Wherever you operate, learn the requirements of your province, state or country in order to operate your driving school successfully.

FEDERAL

In Canada, we also deal with a branch of the Federal Government called the Canada Revenue Agency. They are your silent partner. Any business earning more than thirty thousand dollars per year must register for a Goods and Services Tax (GST) number and render the GST amount on either a quarterly, semiannually or annual basis.

Canada Revenue Agency assesses a penalty for not rendering the GST on time. In other words, they charge you interest for paying late. The same is true for failing to file your yearly personal income statement on time.

If you live in a different country, get in touch with your local authorities for more information.

EPILOGUE

I want to leave you with five ideas to consider while you are on your way to becoming a highly effective driving instructor:

1. Be serious about your work and decide to be the best. Identify the key skills you need to take you to the next level. Attend classes, seminars or conferences in order to develop those skills.

2. Choose your friends and your fellow instructors carefully. Charley Jones said: "You will be in five years the same person you are today, except for the books you read and the people you meet."

3. Take excellent care of yourself. Your body is the only vessel you are granted for this life's journey. You can't exchange it for another one.

4. Always visualize a better version of yourself. "The person you see is the person you will be."

5. Always be action-oriented and no one will be able to predict what is possible for you in your profession.

    - Cover as much ground as you can.

    - Teach as many students as you can.

    - Earn as much money as you can.

According to Brian Tracy:

"The more money you earn,
the more positive and motivated you are,
to see even more people,
to make even more sales,
to make even more money."

Once you become excellent at what you do, you will earn an excellent living for yourself and for your family. You can become one of the most valuable people in your driver training school or your industry. You can make a great difference in the lives of your customers, your industry and your community.

Good luck.

ABOUT THE AUTHOR

Volny Dorcéus is a licensed driving instructor by Alberta Transportation and works as the Senior Instructor for Saint Paul Driving School located in St. Paul, Alberta, Canada.

Volny's education and training include:

- A Business degree from the University of Maine, USA
- A Class 1 Driver's license from Ecole de Transport de Charlesbourg, Quebec, Canada
- A Bachelor of Education degree from Burman University in Lacombe, Alberta, Canada
- A certification in the DISC Model of Human Behavior from Personality Insights, Atlanta, Georgia, USA.

Volny fluently speaks four different languages: Creole, French, English and Spanish.

Volny has been happily married to his wife, Jessy, for the last 25 years. Together they have two adult children, Jack (23) and Marc (22), and an athletic teenager, Ted (14).

Volny travels well over 100,000 kilometers a year in order to provide driver training and personality insights training in the province of Alberta.

OTHER RESOURCES

Brian Tracy, *Eat that Frog! 21 great ways to stop procrastinating and get more done in less time* (Berrett-Koehler Publishers, Inc., 2017)

John C. Maxwell, *Winning With People: Discover the people principles that work for you every time* (Thomas Nelson Publishers, 2004)

Brian Tracy, *Master your time: the breakthrough system to get more results, faster in every area of your life* (Tarcher and Perigee, 2016)

Robert A. Rohm, PhD, *Who do you think you are anyway? How your personality acts, reacts and interacts with others* (Personality Insights Press, 2012)

Steven R Covey, PhD, *The 7 Habits of Highly Effective People* (Free Press, 1989)

Steven R Covey, PhD, *The 8ʰ Habit: From effectiveness to greatness* (Free Press, 2004)

Cheryl Bachelder, *Dare 2 Serve: How to drive superior results by serving others* (Berrett-Koehler Publishers, Inc., 2015)

Brian Tracy, *Unlimited Sales Success: 12 simple steps for selling more than you ever thought possible* (Unabridged audio CD, 2013)

Drs. Travis Bradberry and Jean Greaves, *Emotional Intelligence 2.0* (TalentSmart, 2009)

Learn 2 Change

4903 – 47 St, Box 395, Mirror, AB, T0B 3C0

780-646-0055; 780-806-9289

1learn2change@gmail.com

DESCRIPTION OF
OUR MODULES

Personality development **for teens:**

Get Real! Who you are and why you do those things

In this module, you will learn how to understand yourself by identifying your unique personality style. You will improve your relationships at home, at school, on the job. There is a section on the kinds of work you will find interesting and rewarding and with this information, you will create a plan to put your life together. It's not so much a mystery when you understand yourself and others.

Making sense of your people puzzle

In this module, you will discover how to understand yourself and others.

Adult profile and personality assessment

This profile assessment will help you to understand people in the following areas: their primary drive, their unique giftedness, their value to an organization, their ideal environment, their fears, their response under pressure and their recognition of blind spots.

Individual Personality Dynamics

In this module, you will: know exactly how you are wired, learn issues important to you and others, make wiser decisions, interact more effectively and know how to adjust your personality style.

Interaction Dynamics

In this module, you will learn how to: increase mutual respect, eliminate ongoing conflict, understand how to better meet needs, enhance relationship strengths and develop simple ways to successfully communicate.

Learn 2 Change

4903 – 47 St, Box 395, Mirror, AB, T0B 3C0

780-646-0055; 780-806-9289

1learn2change@gmail.com

Team @ Work – Unlocking your team's potential for better business & relationships

- ✓ Build effective relationships and a more productive team.

- ✓ Learn the value of each team member by understanding the strengths of both the Task-oriented individuals and the People-oriented individuals and how the combination of each personality style influences the team dynamics.

- ✓ Discover the secrets to interacting with your team.

- ✓ Learn about the potential danger zones of your team dynamics.

✓ Discover how to apply insights that will encourage individuals within an organization and utilize each person's talents and abilities for greater productivity and better relationships.

Leadership @ Work – Part 1: Becoming a Dynamic and Effective leader

✓ Gain vital insights towards becoming a great leader and developing even more success with the people you influence.

✓ Identify and develop ways to encourage your team members toward better productivity and team performance.

Leadership @ Work – Part 2: Understanding Needs and Drives in Order to Become a More Effective leader

◆ Learn how to lead more effectively and make better decisions

◆ Know what drives people to action ... performance

◆ How to eliminate barriers to success

◆ Know personal strengths and potential blind spots

◆ Learn ways to improve effectiveness and performance

Conflict resolution @ Work – Adapting your style to create better relationships

- ✓ Understand how personality differences can affect and sometimes create conflict

- ✓ Discover potential danger zones

- ✓ Learn strategies on how to deal with conflict in the workplace

MAXImum
Achievement

Barroom Goary —